**Suicide? Are You Burdened?**
**By the Author Lina M. of Beyond Woman**

Beyond Woman Pty Ltd
PO Box 1018
Sanctuary Cove, Qld, 4212
Australia

Copyright © 2018  Royal Diadem Publishing House Pty Ltd
            Beyond Woman Pty Ltd
            Lina M.

First Edition printed January 2018

Created and designed in Australia.

Scripture taken from the Holy Bible, New International Version®. Copyright © 1973, 1978, 1984, 2011 by International Bible Society.
Used by permission of Zondervan Publishing House. All rights reserved. Italics in Scripture references are for emphasis only.

Beyond Woman is a trademark of Beyond Woman Pty Ltd.

All rights reserved.

# Suicide?
# Are You Burdened?

## Your Journey is Not Yet Over

### By Lina

PO Box 1018
Sanctuary Cove Qld 4212
Australia
Email: seek@royalpublisher.com

**National Library of Australia Cataloguing-in-Publication entry**

Creator: M., Lina, author.

Title: Suicide? are you burdened? : your journey is not yet over / Lina M.

ISBN: 9780994179029 (paperback)

Subjects: Suicide--Prevention.

 Suicide.

# Description

Suicide is a vital element in your life bringing you to a place of decision to make – whether you choose life or death, but life is the solution and substance of your being, comforting your heart with love in motion. So, choose life to overcome death.

Death is your enemy not your friend-- Life on the other hand is your breath and lifeline chosen for you to live and not die.
Death is the enemy of your soul. Choose life in order to grow strong and distribute love and compassion for all who need life.

Overcome fear by choosing life and overcome the destroyer of your soul.

Restrain not your eyes from weeping nor your heart from grieving, but continue to hold onto the will to survive, for you are a free spirit and a survivor in your deepest darkness.

# Guide

| | | |
|---|---|---|
| 1 | The Former is Gone | 11 |
| 2 | You Are Not Alone | 13 |
| 3 | Capture My Heart | 15 |
| 4 | The Comforter Is Here | 19 |
| 5 | Restore Your Mind | 23 |
| 6 | Stop What You Are Doing | 27 |
| 7 | Behold The Future | 31 |
| 8 | Unseen Mercy | 35 |
| 9 | Heart At Peace | 39 |
| 10 | Comfort Your Spirit | 43 |
| 11 | Give Up Not On Yourself | 47 |
| 12 | Live To Survive | 51 |
| 13 | Acknowledge Safety | 55 |

# Guide

| | | |
|---|---|---|
| 14 | Pressure Relieved | **59** |
| 15 | Love Yourself | **63** |
| 16 | Awaken Yourself | **67** |
| 17 | The Future Is Close | **71** |
| 18 | Fulfill Your Destiny | **75** |
| 19 | You Are Not Accused | **79** |
| 20 | Enjoy The Light | **83** |
| 21 | Conquer Death | **87** |
| 22 | Restore The Lost | **91** |
| 23 | Give Up Not On Life | **95** |
| 24 | Anxiety Removed | **97** |
| 25 | Empowering Journey | **101** |

To You My Friends

Neglect Not Thyself

# You Are Not

# On Your Own

# The Former is Gone

Suicide is not the answer nor the solution to any of your problems.

Suicide is a dangerous weapon. Play not with your life nor with danger, for it is a burden that cannot be recovered.

Suicide kills both the mind and the soul of the spirit.

Do not play with danger nor fire-- it is of no value.

Discover yourself in Me, before darkness overshadows your view. Recover your thoughts quickly.

Keep safe and in harmony without giving yourself away.

Look not to danger so that you may not be ensnared by deception. You are loved - spare yourself the agony by resisting the temptation.

2

# You Are Not Alone

Your journey shall first be completed before your days are over.

Why suicide, beloved, and so neglect your calling? Why be led astray by the wicked schemes of the enemy who wants to kidnap your soul, putting ideas in your head that are not of my desires for you?

Forgive those who hurt you, so that you are no longer hurting, upset and in turmoil.

Confusion is not of me, but of the one who is leading you astray.

Help me help you to help others.

By restoring you to your rightful place in my Kingdom, you shall be restored to encourage and help many who are in need of me to be in their lives, for this is your calling.

Look up, I am with you, holding your hand.

3

# Capture My Heart

Calm the stormy weather within your heart, before it becomes an overwhelming feeling in your soul.

Corruption is not of me, for those who are led by the enemy are ruled by him, never to recover again. So do not give into his desires.

Comfort your heart with my love before the ache grows and becomes cancerous.

You are mine; I will not allow the confuser of the brethren to steal, kill and destroy your journey from me.

When you ache, I also ache, and when you are hurting, I am hurting with you too.

Remember your days of old and recall your journey with me-- how we walked side-by-side together along the river of love, the river of delights - the days when you gave me your all.

# Cont... 3

Remember those days-- the time when you boldly faced all your difficulties and patiently waited for me to give you an answer.

You and I danced together closely during the most precious times. You grew up and developed and became the most precious of jewels.

Talk to me once again. I shall not leave you stranded. You are mine in all your fears, confusion and strife.

Keep me in mind before the days are over. It is all about you and your wellbeing. Recover your thoughts quickly before the time runs out and you are unable to think straight.

I, your Healer and great Support, am here to guide you through all your difficulties. Listen to Me: Come out of your own darkness and into the Light that shines upon your face.

# Not Yet Over

Call on me during time of trouble. Call on me during time of need and I shall restore all things lost.

You do not need to slide downhill on that journey, or be led astray by him who despises you - the enemy of your soul, who wants to kidnap your spirit away from your body. Let him not take you.

Hear me, for I am calling your name out loud. Do not do it, do not take your life with your own hands. Call on me for mercy and I will listen and restore you back to life.

Forgive quickly before you are robbed of your life and therefore your beautiful future ahead.

Recover before darkness overrules your heart with corruption and fills your heart with lies. You are to stay safe. Recover quickly and run to my shelter for safety to be spared.

# 4

# The Comforter Is Here

I myself am watching over you. You shall no longer be fighting with anyone, but rather be living in peace.

I have given you another life to live. In my loving care you shall become complete. Hold up, for I am covering you with my presence-- keeping you safe under the shelter of my wings. Therefore, you shall not die but live.

*Thank you, O Creator, thank you for watching carefully over my footsteps that I may live and not die.*

*I want to be with you in heaven, but also desire to continue here on earth. Please have me not be restricted from living and breathing your life.*

*You have called me by name, O God, and I am now answering your call to live and not die.*

# Cont... 4

*I shall give my life to you, rather than to the one who wants to take it away from me - the destroyer of souls.*

*I am a survivor in the arms of Love instead of a weak vessel in the hands of the destroyer.*

*Thank you for showing me the way to Life, rather than death, that I may live and not die. Thank you, O my Heavenly Being.*

*To you, I shall look and by your grace alone I shall live.*

*Take my hand and lead me on, for I have made a decision to remain with you.*

*Here I am alive and well. Halleluiah to you, halleluiah to you, Oh, my Savior, my Deliverer, Restorer of Hope.*

*To you, I give the praise and I am lifted up in glory. Thank you, O Wonderful Counsellor.*

# Grieve No Longer

*Oh, Savior, how I need you, how I need help!*

Why look elsewhere, why look elsewhere, child? Your burdens are my burdens. Come, rest your weary soul upon my shoulder, upon my heart of love and you will find peace like a river and comfort within.

Come, let us travel the world together and enjoy life. Do not despair of life, for I shall hold you up and carry you through the deepest darkness.

You shall not be a slave to the destroyer, for you are seated with me in heavenly places.

Rescue yourself before it is all too late, for the darkness is growing darker in you and you must learn to master it. Take control and overcome it before it takes hold of your being. Let nothing become a stronghold in your life, for the Source of Life lives in you.

# 5

# Restore Your Mind

Feed yourself on the good things from above, not just on the negative thoughts of old.

Unshackle yourself from these unstable chains restricting you before they destroy your mind.

Lighten your burden from within, before you are led astray by destructive thoughts entangling your mind with idol notions.

Enlarge your appetite for more of my Word, that you may have hope without being let down by obstacles and troubling thoughts.

Forgive immediately those who have done you wrong.

Thinking of taking your own life over these issues by being suicidal-- is not really worth it.

Reconsider quickly before time runs out, and you find yourself on the other side - unable to recover, come back or return to the present.

# Cont... 5

I am with you, but first ask for my help before I intervene on your behalf.

I have given you a *will* to make your own choices and decisions based on my Will for you to survive the agony of death; so now choose carefully - choose life not death.

All things can be resolved if you believe - you need not worry. Do not rush to the end of your life. Have a new beginning - a fresh start.

I shall call you home to be with me, but not just yet.

Do not give up on yourself, for the future is bright and waiting to receive you.

Turn and help others be released from their own snares of self-harm, for you are capable.

You are no longer ensnared, but free. Live the real life and prosper in soul, body and mind.

# Do Not Compromise

*Rush to my aid, Oh, my God, Creator of hearts, and spare me from the agony of death, Oh, please... spare me.*

*I rather not be reluctant, but serve you instead and grow to know you.*

*Help me find myself before it is too late, before the storms take over my life and run me down, before the wind blows my vision away.*

*I need you now more than ever before, O Savior.*

I have heard your prayers, child, and I shall save you from agony; but first, you must keep yourself safe and promise to never injure nor kill yourself. Be not burdened by stress, for I am your burden Relief.

Safe in my arms is where I like you to be, safe in my tender embrace forever strong.

# 6

# Stop What You Are Doing

You are not condemned nor shall you ever be. The future is bright. You do not have to take your life on account of these destructive forces entangling your thoughts, twisting your mind and destroying your spirit. Look to Me without wavering, for I have not lost hope in you nor given up on you.

*Oh, Savior of souls, free me from my mentality, from my anxious thoughts that are destroying my heart and keeping me in the realm of darkness. Keep me safe in your loving arms, in your tender embrace, Oh, Restorer of hearts.*

*Oh, Creator, save me from my anxieties, from this overwhelming feeling of distress destroying my vision, and please keep me safe from self-harm and destruction. My memory of you is vivid, but fading away very quickly. Save my soul from pain, agony and sorrow, for to you I call.*

# Cont... 6

*Thank you for hearing my pain and turning my thoughts to you in the right direction, for I wish to live and not die.*

Lift up your soul, O my child, and be not of this world seducing you to destruction. I am your Healer and Deliverer, you shall not be in need of anyone else from here on... for I am your All. Come to your resting arms - Me.

Keep your eyes on the prize and never turn away from your destiny. Look to me and never away from me - your Heavenly Calling.

I shall feed you the eternal Bread of Life - the manna from my Holy Mountain; and from my eternal Rock, satisfy you with water to quench your thirst; and from my Brook with milk and honey, nourish your soul with refreshment.

Never waver in faith. Look up and see me as I really am - your Help and Safety Net.

# You Are Worthy

*Perfect me, O God of my life, Redeemer of hearts, before I die and pass on...*

What are you asking, O my child? This is not the way to be free. Why are you not paying attention to your own life, hoping for the future, believing and caring about your present? The future is not demanding much from you... only that you live it well.

Eternity awaits your arrival, but not just yet. Falter not during time of trouble and despair, instead be strengthened in spirit that you may pass the test of time. Dwell beside my still waters of safety, without wavering or giving up. Have no form of confusion, for I am your All - you can rely on me.

To you I call; will you listen and heed my voice calling your name to be safe - I am with you. See yourself through the eyes of love and walk with freedom.

# 7

# Behold The Future

I love you, child, I do love you. Turn to me with all your heart and let not the enemy snatch your thoughts away from me, to kidnap your soul from my Kingdom of mercy.

Neglect not your faith, for you have believed, therefore, you now receive. Complete your journey here on earth and do not give up on yourself nor give your life away to another.

My love for you remains loyal, faithful, and true. You are the apple of my eye, beloved - the life I breathed into existence.

Know me for who I am, before the night captures your heart and snatches you away. I am loyal to you. Do not be robbed of the life you first journeyed here on earth with me.

Let not the enemy of your soul connive you with thoughts that do not count. I am the One who looks after your need. Now be free.

# Cont... 7

O beloved, you are so precious to me, child. Feed yourself on my Will to be able to live and withstand these times of sorrow. Turn to me with all your heart and consider not death.

The beauty of life is that you can choose to live.

*Thank you for seeing me through my difficulties, O, my Guiding Light, thank you for your love. Teach me how to soar with you on the Mountain Top like an eagle, rather than take my own life and die. Capture my spirit to save my soul.*

I am right here with you, beloved, standing beside you, on your side.

*Take my life into your hands, O God of my life, and redeem me by drawing me closer to your side. I need you, Oh, how... I so need you.*

Look my way, child - away from all confusion.

# Soul Provider

*Direct my footsteps in you, O my Creator, direct my heart to move along with you. May I rest in your Will of love and consider all my steps.*

*I feel neglected and unable to get up - defeated and not strong. I desire to live and not die; but my heart beats courageously towards death, for at present I do not feel so entangled by grace. I am at a crossroad, and need to make a choice either to follow my own deadly way of sorrow or your Life of goodness to me from the inside-out. I honor your ways, but I am also led astray. Help me know you, O my eternal destiny, and take over my disturbance, for without you, I am dead anyway. I desire to see myself entangled by grace and not have this feeling of death niggling at me. Help, O please help.*

Corruption is not of me, child. My Will for you is to live happily and not die sadly.

8

# Unseen Mercy

No one can take you away from me, beloved, for I am your Source of life - Your Beginning and very Last, if you choose me to be!

I shall open the floodgates of heaven over your life once you have made a decision to turn to Me and not away from Me.

I shall consolidate you, as you turn your face and your back towards me.

I shall restore what the locusts have eaten by comforting your heart in me, as you surrender your all to me. I shall also show you the way of righteousness by your actions of truth.

Come to know me, for I shall support you in comfort as you rest your burdened heart upon my shoulder.

I am on your side; turn nor left nor right, rather keep your focus on me - Your Eternal Guarantee.

# Cont... 8

I only desire the best for you, child. Choose my comfort and support rather than listening to your own mind and frame of thought - I am the spirit within you who leads you on.

*Thank you, Oh, my precious Light, for loving me enough by turning me to you.*

*I am willing and able to return to my rightful place with you, my family and friends. I shall look to no other, but only to you and be thankful to all that I have with you.*

*Thank you for unshackling me from all this misery and crime, which I nearly brought upon myself.*

Beloved child, he who loves you Am here.

You do not need to go through this agony. Release yourself by coming to me willingly.

Journey on... Oh, my precious one.

# Journey On Soldier

*Touch my core and renew my mind, O my Creator. Renew my spirit, that I may master my thoughts and move forward to a better place. Complete my journey here with you, that I may be mesmerized by your grace. Entangle me that I may not be detangled from this journey of love bestowed upon me. You have placed your hand upon my head and saved me. Now Oh, Healer of my soul, heal me, heal my core from being led astray from your Will to see me safe. My story must be told, though not when I am dead, but while I'm still alive and living.*

*Thank you for detangling me from reckless living and negative thoughts that were disturbing me. Thank you for assuring me safety to journey on. Give me the victory before I decide to go the way of no return and ruin my life completely.*

Child, you have it all in Me - just rest.

9

# Heart At Peace

*I shall not turn my back to you, Oh, God of my fathers, for you have held me close to your heart since my youth and saved me on multiple occasions from the snares set before me by the enemy of my soul. Although he connives and steals all day long, he has no power over me. He is a dead beast as far as I am concerned, wasted and wasting others along with him. I shall look to no one else to save me but you. Help me, Oh, Giver of Life... help me... help me, Oh, my Guiding Light - Angel of Life.*

Help others, child. Help redeem the lost, rather than waste your precious life listening to the enemy, who has nothing good to say.

Do not listen to the voice of him whose aim is to rob and snatch your life away from me. Kill the desire to die by living in me, and destroy the schemes of the enemy who is tormenting your soul... torturing your spirit.

# Cont... 9

Rest from his wrongdoing by coming to me - your Life.

DO NOT LISTEN TO HIS WORDS, NOR RECEIVE HIS SENSES THAT WORK IN YOU AT TIMES.

Do not indulge in that which is evil and conniving, misleading and entrapping.

*I will, O Lifter of my head, I will... Thank you for watching over me.*

I am from Everlasting to Everlasting - your God, whose love is here to benefit you.

*I acknowledge you, Oh, my Creator - Restorer of lives. I call to you at this time and I am saved from my agony - set free from my misery. Thank you for loving me, thank you for beholding me. I am acknowledged... thank you. I shall live and not die.*

# Return Home

You are not left in the dark, the way it may seem to you right now, but you are my honor on earth to sing my praises all day long.

You have not asked me to help you nor support you, but you need to. You do not need to cry on your own without asking for my help.

*I need you, O Savior; I need you forever. Train me, teach me your ways of truth, that I may walk in them and never stumble nor fall.*

Renew your mind, son, renew your heart, that you may undress yourself from thoughts that are torturing your spirit and recover quickly by abiding in me, for I do know that which is best for you. You shall not be left stranded, for my grace abounds and shall lift you up in glory.

*Thank you for loving me and giving me another chance to live, O my loving Savior.*

# 10

# Comfort Your Spirit

*I shall count it all a loss, O my Creator; I shall count it all a loss when I am gone from this world of agony and sorrow. Sorry that I could not make it, for I am disturbed, filled with grief and deeply troubled. I am crying, for I have no one to lift me up from this miserable feeling of entanglement. I desire to be free, but have no refuge - no home to call my own. I am in strife and cannot escape. I need someone to understand me and give me the courage to move on, but there is none.*

Child, Oh, my beloved child, the power of my Kingdom shall support you, and the grace of my love shall empower you.

Why don't you just carry on as you have always and wait for the results to speak for themselves on your behalf? You are capable. Just walk in the direction chosen for you, and you will see my right hand of power displayed.

# Cont... 10

Commission your soul not to be disturbed, O child; commission your soul to live on... I shall uphold you by my loving arms and carry you through in love. You are not to leave this earth yet, for it is not your time nor my Will for you.

*Save me that I may not stray, O my God of love. You have looked after me in the past, and I am in need of you now to watch over me. I am about to harm myself and need your guiding light to support me.*

*Watch over me, Oh, watch over me, for I need you to recover me so desperately, before time steals me away from you and my family. I am trusting in you to look after me. Guard me, and by your grace, O please, recover me.*

Child, my grace is sufficient for you in time of weakness.

# Listen To My Heart

Recall the days of old and follow me. Be drawn to your thoughts of love and compassion. Lean not on the voice of the enemy who suppresses. Retreat not, nor give up on yourself, for what I have for you is far greater than these things telling you otherwise. You mean more to me than you now know.

I have called you by grace that you may know me in Love. Come to me before the night is over, for my Will for you is to survive. Child, you are not to journey down that road, but be lifted up instead.

*Savior, I am reluctant to turn and come to you at a time like this. I feel devoted to my natural instincts leading me astray to my death bed. I do not want to give in, but as if I have no other choice-- it seems to be my only way out.*

Be careful not to make rash decisions, child.

ed # 11

# Give Up Not On Yourself

I hope that you would not be displeasing to me, child. Give up on those impulses that are telling you otherwise - those forces that are supporting the darkness rather than the Light.

I am here to help free you from all these negative impulses.

Do not go the other way - the way of death, rather die to self that you may truly live.

I have called you by name that you may live and not die the death of the wicked.

Honor my Name by the grace and love given you. I am your Alpha and Omega, the Beginning and the End of your time.

Look up to me and do not give way to disaster, for it is not of Me.

You are not to choose the way of death, but the way of Life instead. Neglect not yourself.

# Cont... 11

*Oh, my Loving Savior, help me surrender my will to your Will, that I may live to enjoy the benefits without restraint.*

Sure, my beloved, sure... Keep me in mind and you will be strengthened to live on.

Now live happily before me and give up not on yourself.

I am your Everlasting Peace. Come to me and fret not.

*O my Savior in time of distress; you are my Shepherd during the lonely times in the wilderness, my Protector from the desert heat. Help me quickly, Oh, God of my life. I want to be one with Life rather than death. Help me surrender to you instead... help me.*

Be not anywhere else, beloved, except in my loving arms of tenderness supporting you to carry on in love.

# Prepare For The Days Ahead

Recover quickly from those thoughts that are telling you otherwise. Quickly remove yourself from the snare. Be unshackled before the journey is shortened and robbed from you forever.

Be not consumed by trouble, for it is not doing you any good. Release yourself quickly without any hesitation. Burden not yourself, for I am the one who saves you.

The snares of death shall not entangle you - you are an overcomer. Live and not die - breathe life not death. Include Me in all you do without wavering or having any feelings of distress.

*Thank you for being my Guide, my great Support. Thank you for reassuring me help and supporting me in your loving kindness. O God of my heart, thank you for not giving up on me.*

# 12

# Live To Survive

*My life is in the palm of your hand, O God of my soul. Look my way and do not turn away from me, I ask, for I need you so desperately.*

*Lead others on the same path of forgiveness, for there is no one that cares for them. Only you can I turn to, only to you can I run and feel safe. I have suffered much and only in you can I run with freedom.*

Burden not yourself, beloved, for I have heard your prayers and assured you salvation.

I shall restore the times spent together during the time of loneliness.

You do not need to wail on your death bed any longer, for I have created you to live.

Run away from this torture tormenting your soul, and grieve over those who are lost in spirit rather than over opportunities missed.

# Cont... 12

The time of my forgiveness has come for all who are willing to repent from their past sins.

Confusion is not of me nor should you partake of it yourself.

I am on your side in all things. I can turn your dry river into a vast sea; your flood of tears into a peaceful stream, and give you the Water of Life in exchange for your desert season. All you have to do is look to me and ask for anything you so wish and I will waste no time in giving you that which is best for you.

The way to heaven can only be approved by me - your Savior and Guiding Light. Love yourself enough to never leave this earth before your time.

I love you, do not be entangled by corruptive thoughts disturbing your mind to end it. Save yourself from death and run towards Life.

# Call For Help

*Complete my mission before all is lost, Oh, my Creator of hearts, for by myself I can do nothing - with you all things are made possible.*

*Thank you, O Lord, King of the universe, for who you are within me. My mother and father have said that I am not good enough, but I know in you all things are made possible. Turn me around to succeed, accomplish, and become all that you desire for me to be. Fulfill my destiny, I ask.*

Beloved, you are complete, pure and innocent. Nothing should ever be too hard or difficult for you to accomplish. I have given you the victory - walk in it.

In Me, you have a way out. Run away from all this confusion suppressing your soul and come away with me. Fall into my loving arms of grace supporting you.

# 13

# Acknowledge Safety

Child, the future is bright. Why ruin your life by death? Why not take advantage of the real life offered to you instead?

Do not listen to those voices tormenting you from within. Rather look to your Maker, who bore you and looked after your wellbeing all those years you were in the womb of the earth.

I looked after you and nourished you. Do you now wish to be led astray by a voice that is not of me? Do you wish to turn away from me and give your life to the evil one who wants you dead rather than alive?

Your behavior should be that of my Kingdom, not of the one who is torturing your soul with thoughts that are corrupt-- such as death, turmoil and confusion. Look away from those thoughts that are corrupting your mind, for they are not of me nor sent to you from heaven by me.

# Cont... 13

Rekindle the Fire from within and run with the Wind of my Spirit to the furthest places available, where you can rest together with me in total harmony.

I love you, child. Love is your answer to every question and every solution holding you back. Be real to be yourself and no longer drink confusion like water. I am on your side - be enlightened.

*Thank you for giving me the grace to go on, O my Gracious King.*

Yes, beloved, I have called you by name and raised you up by grace. Now do yourself a favor and do not self-harm - you will be pleased that you never did.

*Thank you for your wisdom, Oh, Creator of my being. You are Love, and without you I can not survive. You are the True Word of Life.*

# Gain Not Lose

*Oh, Redeemer of souls, I can no longer tolerate my wrongdoing. I have injured many people and resisted correction. I no longer know what to do... Help me, I ask.*

Your will should be my Will, O son of righteousness, for I am the One beholding you in glory.

Shine like the angels, rather than die out like a candle in the night. Look up and rekindle the flames without any fear, doubt or confusion. Rest, child, for your future is found in Me. Rejoice without thoughts of suicide and be free from this pressure oppressing you.

Complete your mission before your vision is lost. Test me and see. I shall open the windows of Heaven over your life and set you free. You may ask me for anything, and that I shall do for you. Since you have asked, you shall now receive.

# 14

# Pressure Relieved

Why choose death over life when you can choose to live, O my beloved child? Why? Why do you want to give yourself over to the other side, instead of joining me? Why do you want to suffocate yourself in this manner? Why look to death for answers, when you can seek Faith to live instead? Why forbid yourself? Why destroy your freedom by submitting to an instinct that serves no purpose - except destroys? Why keep up your courage with falsehood, rather than believe in me to take you away from all this clamor hovering over your life? Why not lead others into my way of righteousness and lead a good example for them to follow? Why burden yourself and so be in distress? Why not come to me for answers instead of occupying yourself with deceit from the deceiver, who has no mercy on you or on anyone else? Are you listening? Are you truly listening? I am here waiting, ready to hear you voice.

# Cont... 14

Oh, child, are you listening? Are you truly listening to my words of love and encouragement, that you may benefit twice.

Be comforted in my Truth of Love and you will recover.

Is your heart in the right place, that I may cradle you in love and hold you close to my heart of compassion? Are you wondering what I am saying to you? Will you co-operate with me? Do you want to come home to be with me? Do you want to run the race with me? Will you give yourself wholeheartedly to me? Will you rest your burdened heart on my shoulder of love?

Feel not deserted, Oh... child, for you are not. You are loved beyond measure, O my blessed one. Be comforted and rest your weary soul upon my shoulder of grace, ready to support you.

# The Future Awaits

*Oh, God of all creation, how I honor your Name, but right now I am confused and unsure of many things.*

Journey on, child, journey on, and bring forth new thoughts that are appealing and pleasant.

I am your Anchor of Hope, your Word of Truth, Best Friend and Love Divine.

May my Will be done in your life, and my love capture your heart. In me, you have discovered yourself and were given the Sword of Victory. I have empowered you to destroy kingdoms and thrones, and you demolished every stronghold and opposition that raised its ugly head against you.

Return to your Maker, to your supporting grace and belief. Capture my heart in spirit and be united. Walk in the freedom you know, so that you may be released from complications.

# 15

# Love Yourself

The vision of tomorrow must be completed today.

You shall turn to me without wavering, for I have beheld your cause without shattering your soul.

Keep safe in my loving arms, for I am your Heavenly host, the Father for all eternity. My Name is written on your forehead, just as your name is engraved in the palm of my hand.

*Keep me safe, O Deliverer of mankind. Keep me redeemed in your loving care. Although you have kept me safe for many years, I feel as though I want to die now, for my hope of tomorrow has vanished.*

Child, Oh, sweet child of mine. I want to give you today, that you may have another day to live tomorrow. Just as tomorrow must come, so you too must also remain alive today.

# Cont... 15

*Oh, God of my life, the heart of me cries out to you, just as your spirit yearns to set me free. You have saved me on many occasions, and when you called I listened; but today I am overly burdened and troubled-- my grief is beyond measure, beyond description and solution. Redeem me I pray, redeem me before I faint from sorrow and grief. I am overwhelmed with stress and not released. My heart is pounding severely and I am in agony. Save me, O God of love and mercy, save me.*

O child, the well is deep, and you are to drink from the River of Life. Rest in me that I may give you hope for a new day. The hope of tomorrow must be released today.

*Complete me, O Maker of heaven, and change my way of thinking-- my mind, my soul, my image, that I may be restored back to Life.*

# Do Not Injure Yourself

*Feel me, Oh, Lifter of souls, and fill me with your love, that I may share with others all your goodness to me, for to you I call and give my all.*

Child, you are not to be in need of anyone else but Me, for I am the One who makes all your plans succeed.

I know others have stolen from you, but I am here to restore every loss. Develop character and not crime. Act on faith and not fear, for I am your Assured Victory. The Future shall see you through, for you are not on your own. I myself am with you and on your side completely.

*Oh, Great Deliverer, how I honor you.*

Burn with zeal for my house, son, which is my body, rather than destroy that which I have created, so I may live and dwell in you.

# 16

# Awaken Yourself

*O God of my life, I am crying and grieving, needing and pleading; disturbed and forever looking to you for help and support.*

Beloved child, enjoy your time with me before all is lost.

*How can I, Oh, my Savior? I have lost the one I love. The one who gave me hope to live together my future with you and be united to you in love. I have lost my special one, and choose not to live any longer, but desire to die, for my heart aches at their departure. I miss them dearly and desire to be with them urgently. My heart is not released, and I am overwhelmed by struggles. I am bound to my loved one, for they are one with me and part of me. I desire to be with them and be burden released. Help me see the Light of Life. Please watch over my soul, for I am afraid and desire to be free from this torture consuming me.*

# Cont... 16

*Thoughts come and go. They may displease you and be displeasing to my soul as well, but where can I find rest without the one I have lost? They have given me hope to live, but now I feel like an empty shell and stranded. I feel I want to die rather than live.*

Hope, beloved; hope, is the greatest treasure for survival - the blessed life to reassure faith. Be encouraged, I am your Will to survive. I give you power to remain alive, to love and live on. As for your loved ones, leave them to me. I shall see both of you in heaven with me, and do that which is best for your eternity.

*I desire to recover, Oh, God of my life. Lead me I ask. Thank you for who you are to me.*

I am willing, beloved child - be recovered, healed and restored. I am your Destiny and Eternal Future - keep that in mind and recover the loss by continuing to be alive.

# Redeemed for Life

Be not reluctant to run the race marked out for you, child. Do not waste any more time on thoughts that kill the body and grieve the spirit. Concern not yourself with the attitudes of others. Allow my Word to free you from thoughts that are not of me but of the world. Confuse not your soul with your spirit, instead keep a clear mind intact at all times. I am the Alpha and the Omega of your life... reject not my favor upon your future.

Neglect not yourself by taking your life with your own hands, rather leave room for my wrath to avenge you from all your enemies and free you from their deep oppression. Consider carefully; do not give way to your enemy - the destroyer of souls and act not on impulse.

I shall see you through your feelings of hopelessness. Reconsider to prosper and walk forth. Believe in yourself.

# 17

# The Future Is Close

Cry out from the heart, O you mighty warrior. Stand tall and let nothing move you, for you are the child of my being.

Grieve no longer, for the battles you fought were not on your own - I counted them with you. You endured and escaped the destroyer of souls - who is bent on evil.

I have welcomed you into my kingdom of grace by choice and not by control. Your kingly anointing is faithful and remains irrevocable.

Today is a new day for you and it must end on a good note. Do nothing out of place as to hurt yourself. I have given you tomorrow and the future we shall behold together.

You are to anchor yourself in me in complete harmony. No need for stress nor any form of strife and confusion, for I am the Lifter of your soul, the One who makes you whole.

# Cont... 17

I am encouraging you to live and not die. My Word shall lift you up and not burden you.

You have proved faithful, therefore I have kept an open door of escape for you - by my Will through my Word of Life encouraging you.

Child, look up, and you shall find me. Release your burdens and touch me. Keep safe under the shadow of my wings and you will not be burdened.

*O my Guiding Light, by your saving grace I am healed.*

Now, child of love, complete your journey and do not think of past experiences entangling your thoughts with bad memories.

The old is no longer suited, for the new has taken over. Walk in freedom, for I have given you a new journey to begin and start afresh.

# Face Reality

Do not injure yourself, Oh, my child.

*O my Creator, the future is no longer in my hands, for there is nothing else left for me. I call to you, but you don't seem to hear nor listen to my plea. Where are you when I need you? Oh, my Savior Redeemer, you who call yourself my friend. I am so confused and crying out for someone to reach my dying heart, hear my voice and respond, but there is none, there is no one to help me nor support me. Therefore, I now choose to die rather than live and run away from any and every responsibility.*

Beloved, remain calm and calculated. Do not rush into such a decision, which you then cannot retrieve. You do not need to put your life in catastrophe, for the Love within you shall support you. Lose not your foothold to death, nor give yourself over to the darkness surrounding your thoughts.

# 18

# Fulfill Your Destiny

The One who saves is here. Look to me and you shall find me right here beside you.

Do not let your will defy that which is best for you, for truly I have given you hope and a future - now walk in it.

Act on that which is best for you, not on those thoughts that are deadly and conniving... deceiving your mind, telling you otherwise.

*Restore me to my rightful place, Oh, Redeemer. Restore me and help me cross over from death to life. I desire to die, but also want to live to make a difference.*

*Help me surrender myself to you eternally.*

My favor upon your life, child, is your security, just as my Word to you is true.

*I shall look to no other, except to you, O my God of Grace.*

# Cont... 18

*Thank you, O God of my life, for enlightening my soul to move forward with you.*

*I have reached a level of understanding to know what the enemy of disaster is doing and what I need to be doing. Thank you.*

*I now give myself to you completely. Thank you for not giving up on me.*

Beloved child, you are the apple of my eye and the future of my desires fulfilled - my eternal purpose. I desire for you to recover quickly from this situation tormenting your spirit.

Beloved, do not throw away that which is good for you, for success is just around the corner.

Rejoice, for the angels of heaven are supporting you during your weakest moments.

Arise and shine. Come out of your affliction, Oh, dear one.

# Forgiveness Released

*Oh, Savior of my soul, you are the key to my heart, but right now I am in need of your touch. I am wavering in faith by the thoughts that are accumulating in me.*

*The future with you is assured, but my will without you is not. I feel distorted and confused. Recover me, O recover me, that I may not fall asleep. Recover me that I may see the Light and walk in victory.*

*Hold me close to you that I may see the Light of Life and be redeemed. In your loving arms is where I desire to be. Keep me safe that I may fulfill your purpose in my life and not injure myself with my own hands.*

*You are the Giver of life and with you there is safety. Keep me safe that I may know your Will and teach my children the way of safety. I need no one else but you, for you are the God of my eternity.*

# 19

# You Are Not Accused

Accuse not yourself - I am your Judge, just as I am your Great Reward. Turn to me, for I shall lift you up from your misery.

You are called to enlighten others; but do not destroy yourself in the process.

*Savior of my soul, I have had enough of this world and situations that are torturing my soul and telling me to fade away and die. What am I to do? All is lost, all counts for nothing!*

*I believe in your Word and in all that is good, but then I disbelieve... I agree with you, and then I disagree. What sorrow have I brought upon myself! Rescue me from this misery that I may smell the roses once again and settle in a place of peace.*

Help yourself escape, O my beloved child, by believing in yourself. You have my approval.

# Cont... 19

*You are my Alpha and Omega and to you I am grateful. Thank you for your support; thank you for taking me out of this muddied water, which is diluting my thoughts towards you.*

*I am a conqueror, and I shall not give myself to another except to you. Thank you for holding me close to your love.*

*The future I behold with you, Oh, my Redeemer and Best Friend, for the race is not for the swift nor the battle for the strong, but for Him who loves you.*

*I am thankful that my days are not in my hands. Help me number my days and be wise in my decisions.*

*Thank you for my Life, O God of Grace, you who loved me first. Oh, Love Divine; thank you for saving me from death and giving me a happy life instead.*

# Concealed Faith

*Savior of my soul, Redeemer of my spirit, my burden is not of you, nor should it be counted; only love should live in me, for you are my never-ending story. Yes, you are my burden Relief in time of trouble - The Creator of all things - The One, who lives in me.*

*Oh, Savior, you have comforted my heart and redeemed my spirit from the snare. You have made me your home and given me the victory. My Refuge is you; my will is your Will; my name is found in you, and my life is also discovered in you - I am yours for all eternity.*

Child, keep your head up and your face shining through the deepest darkness.

I believe in you. Let your *will* become mine and survive to live. Be not discouraged in any way, for you need to live to love, just as you need to forgive in order to love, and love to live in the forgiveness of truth.

# 20

# Enjoy The Light

*O God of Love, I desire to lead a good life and set an example for others to follow; rather than the idiot I have been - neglecting your power of love from ruling and reigning over me.*

*Thank you for restoring me back to health and watching over my every step. Thank you, that you do restore all things lost and give us joy.*

*Now, I look to you for everything, for you are the One I adore. My calmness is found in you, and my heart is discovered with you.*

I love you, child, now leave all these dramas behind, and walk confidently in the freedom given you.

*You are the only one I see, Oh, my God of Creation. Thank you for freeing me from the snare that nearly took my life away from you, and my loved ones.*

# Cont... 20

*Mercy... mercy me... I look to you for mercy, and I am not disregarded, for you are my Renewal and Eternal Reward.*

*Protect me from going back to my old ways of doing things, for I desire to remain with you and never look back. I do not wish to return to my old ways and patterns that are not of you. Oh, God of love.*

Child, the answers are within you, within your own heart. Listen and run towards the Light, which is shining upon your face even now.

Look not back to your old style of living. Keep it behind you and move on forward towards your calling. You are free from pressure.

Give me the praise as you do, for I am in this place here with you. I shall see you through every difficulty. Open up your eyes and see all that I have destined for you.

# Pure Thoughts

I shall honor you, son, as you make the right decisions to follow my Word of Love and encouragement. Walk in my ways and never let go of your Greatest Support - Me.

Recover quickly, before you are taken away from the earth. Recover your thoughts, before it is too late for you to think straight.

The Giver of Life I am, and I shall not see you waste your life away to the enemy through death. Recover quickly that you may find peace and be released from his snare entrapping your soul.

I am on your side; do not mingle the Good with the bad.

*King of love, help me surrender before all is gone... before all is lost. I hand over to you my body, soul and spirit. Redeem me, Oh, God of mercy, so that I may not die but live.*

# 21

# Conquer Death

Keep up your courage, Oh, my child, keep up your courage.

Have me see you turn your life around... have me see you turn.

Rejoice in me, daughter, and do not waste your precious life away.

Call on me in time of trouble that I may hear your voice and hold your hand.

Your future is more important than your present circumstances, so take my hand and be led by my spirit.

*Thank you, O Savior of souls, for being my example of love. Thank you for being my Friend and Eternal Guide.*

Eternally I am yours. Give me your heart, child, and run away to be with me in a place where no one else knows.

# Cont... 21

I am waiting to meet you, waiting to reward you for all the good you have done. Now continue and never give up on WHO YOU ARE in ME.

*I understand, I now fully understand, O God of my being. Therefore, I shall now turn my life over to you and glorify your Holiness through praise.*

Seek me, seek life and live, O my child.

*Purify my heart that my thoughts might be purified, for to you, I surrender, O my God of life. I shall live and not die, for you have given me hope and a future.*

Love yourself first, Oh, my child, and never compromise your life in exchange with death. Die to self daily instead, that you may enjoy an abundant life and prosper in all your ways. I am on your side completely.

# Be Awakened

Run and do not stop running my way, for I shall take care of your every need by fulfilling your every desire asked of me.

*Forgive me, O loving God, Redeemer of lives, forgive me for neglecting myself and tearing myself to pieces. Forgive my hidden faults and reassure me life, for I am in need of your favor.*

*Savior of lives, I have heard your Word and taken great delight in your wisdom.*

*Restore me I pray and lead me in the way I should go, that I may grow in love and learn how to forgive. I ask that you would heal my broken heart and lead me when it is time, to my everlasting peace.*

Child, you are forgiven, and I release you into my Realm of Love. Surrender your all to Me - Your Life by turning away from death.

# 22

# Restore The Lost

*Oh loving Creator, I can no longer take these burdens troubling me upon my own shoulders.*

*Help me surrender to life than die and waste away to nothing. You have given your life to me, and I want to share it with the world. My sin you have wiped away, and the key of victory you have given me.*

*I belong to you and to no other, for you have set my spirit free.*

*Thank you for loving me. Thank you for the greatness of your love upon my life, for the whisper of your sound within me and the love we share together for all eternity. You have given me a hope and a future, and to you my face I turn, for from now on my back the world shall only see.*

Child, lift up your head, for you are not alone.

# Cont... 22

*I have shut the door on every negative thought disturbing me, for with you I have found my destiny.*

Be not disturbed, child, for I am with you - holding your hand.

Look not away from Life, for I shall see you through all your difficulties - especially at a time like this.

Retreat from the thoughts of death. You are a survivor.

Remove every negative decision based on death by replacing it with lively thoughts.

Do not be weakened by circumstances made to test you.

Seek to live instead of choosing death over your life. You are free from confusion-- run for your life, and take cover in me.

# Turn Around

You are victorious, child, you do not need to think dark thoughts. Just believe in yourself and come to know who you really are.

I have called you by name and rebirthed you into love by giving you a new heart to share with everyone. Why submit to another other than me? Why give into death when you can have Life? You are not to be afraid any longer. Have faith to live the righteous life required. Why be led astray by vicious thoughts disturbing you, rather than the will to survive? I have empowered you to be an overcomer. Rest in my love, for I am your Guiding Light.

Do not turn away from all that I have taught you and so do away with your Maker. You are not on your own; others are having the same thoughts as you; and you are to help them.

Do not burden yourself by following their steps of death; rather, retreat by choosing Life.

# 23

# Give Up Not On Life

*Complete me in you, Oh, God of my being, Creator of my life, for in you I have found my refuge and I will never waver in faith, nor ever turn away from serving you.*

*Forgive my hidden faults, O my Sovereign, and restore my faith in you, for you have shown me love and given me hope.*

*To whom must I turn, if not to you? You are the Lover of my soul, my burden Relief, the Sensor of my spirit and my Source of Life. Complete me that I may be restored, I ask.*

*Forgive me that I may be healed. Teach me your ways that I might be moved by your spirit and never turn away from you.*

*You are my healing hands. You have given me many gifts - may I use them all wisely.*

*I am watching over you, carefully, O child, and holding your hand joyfully - be resurrected.*

# 24

# Anxiety Removed

*Capture my heart, Oh, King of my spirit, that I may walk in your likeness and forget these troubled times. I desire to lay them all down, put them behind me, lay them to rest and never look back. I wonder if my time is up, Oh, Giver of life, I wonder if my time is up.*

Child, the choice is yours, but I urge you to restrain from negative thoughts that do no one any good.

*I am calling out to you, O Savior of my spirit; rush to my aid, for I am about to take my life.*

O child, I encourage you to turn to me and not away from me. You shall prosper much, if you do not give into these thoughts accusing you falsely and entangling your spirit with all kinds of negative notions. Listen to me and do not turn a deaf ear to the voice within you-- calling you out of the darkness into the Light. Be released from this snare entangling you."

# Cont... 24

Release yourself quickly and be set free from the snare of death by my victory, for He who loves you has set you free for all eternity.

I am your cup of Life. Destroy death by living the Life of Love. Capture the light, that you may know who I really am to you, beloved.

Delay not, rather run by turning around to me... Now... Now... Now.

Loving you always. Free yourself and come to me without any delay or second thoughts.

Your mother is waiting to see you again, and your father is calling you home.

Keep running the race of life marked out for you without wishing to be dead, but rather alive. Keep your eyes set on the goal.

You have been redeemed by grace in love.

# Benefit Yourself

Tell your soul to live on and accomplish my purpose, beloved child.

*Heal me, I ask, O Healer of broken hearts, and teach me your decrees that are supporting me. Bless me with your will power that I may resist the temptation of taking my own life.*

*You created me to serve you and from the grave empowered me to rule over the enemy whom you crushed underfoot.*

*You O Lord, are my burden Relief, Conqueror, Support Stream of Love for all Eternity.*

*Redeem me from my anxious thoughts, I pray, that I may live your life of love wholeheartedly, and become not entangled by the snares of society entrapping my thoughts and disregarding me.*

*Behold me in your glory, I ask and pray, for to you I turn and am helped.*

# 25

# Empowering Journey

*My thoughts of you, O God of my life, are pleasant thoughts, but destructive forces are entangling my memories and reuniting me to death. I desire to live and not die, but am not strong enough to survive the tormenting experiences of society telling me otherwise.*

*I am injured in soul and compelled by choice to do what I must - what I see fit. I am conquered in spirit and overwhelmed in heart. My mind is becoming confused.*

*Turn me, Oh, turn me, quickly, O Savior of mankind, and never let me go, for I need you urgently. May I recover quickly from these tormenting thoughts accusing me falsely. To you, I turn; help me... I pray.*

Yes, child, run to me for cover and hide yourself under the shadow of my wings, for I am your Source, your Saving Grace.

# A Prayer

# From The Heart

# Help Me

*Comfort my heart O God of love and no longer see me come to ruin like this, for my heart is unstable and mind is captured by thoughts not letting me be.*

*I ask for your deliverance and pray for your healing over my mind, body, soul, spirit and finances that are in ruin over my thoughts disturbing me.*

*Help me I pray and let me be I ask. Help me know what to do in a situation like this and be set free to run the race marked out for me.*

*My life is in your hands O God, direct it as you please, for I am exhausted and tired of suffering the consequences of my affliction.*

*Help me by supporting me and take over my life and forgive me for neglecting you - my very Life Breath. Support me I ask and pray, for I need you.*

# Redeem Me

*O God of love and compassion, I need you to set me free from my misery, for I am burdened and no longer standing strong. Keep me safe that I may withstand a chance, without a ruin or any form neglect or misery.*

*I need your helps so desperately. Help me I pray, that I may be freed up and no longer a burden to anyone else.*

*I desire to live and not die, for I have so much to offer everyone who is need, but I must be freed first without anyone hurting me any longer. So, help me I pray.*

*I no longer want to be seduced by death, but by life tempting me. I pray for your deliverance from these thoughts entangling my ways, ruining my mind and seducing me to do wrong to myself by killing me. I need your help to free me completely and no longer torment me.*

*Lead me in the Way of Truth, I pray.*

# Capture My Heart

*Help O God of nations, help me know your will and walk in your ways of love, that I may understand how to love myself and become one with my spirit of faith in action supported by grace.*

*Neglect not your calling O my child of grace, but keep to a path away from death and cross over to life watching over you so carefully. Be not detangled from that which is good and honorable, but rather stay away from everything that ruins your life and robs you of the victory. Contention will not support you, nor negative thoughts of yourself, will enhance, Oh, child. So run with me and carry my burden of saving lives not putting them to death by the sword destroying their soul by negative thoughts oppressing them by fear, turmoil and neglect.*

*Oh, God, hear my voice and help me see myself through your eyes of love I pray.*

*Support me I ask, and hear my heart cry.*

## The Love of the Father
*Neglect not Yourself*

★ *Psa 38:22* **Come quickly to help me, my Lord and my Savior.**

*Psa 142:1* **I cry aloud to the Lord; I lift up my voice to the Lord for mercy.**

*Joh 3:14* **So if the Son sets you free, you will be free indeed.**

# The Power of Love
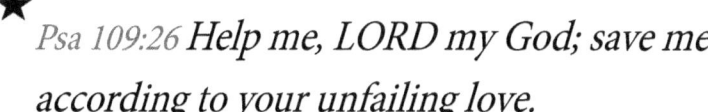

★ *Psa 109:26* **Help me, LORD my God; save me according to your unfailing love.**

*Psa 109:21* **But you, Sovereign LORD, help me for your name's sake; out of the goodness of your love, deliver me.**

*Zec 5:5*... **Look up and see what is appearing."**

# A NEW BEGINNING

# A NEW JOURNEY

Check out our range of exciting and motivational new **B**eyond **W**oman® books, inspirational music, irresistible fragrance and selection of empowering products!

www.MyBeyondWoman.com

facebook.com/AuthorLinaM

facebook.com/BeyondWoman

facebook.com/MyBeyondWoman

twitter.com/MyBeyondWoman

instagram.com/MyBeyondWoman

youtube.com/MyBeyondWoman

www.ingramcontent.com/pod-product-compliance
Lightning Source LLC
Chambersburg PA
CBHW070542300426
44113CB00011B/1756